Poetic Confinement

By Darick "DDS" Spears

Poetic Confinement

Written and "UN-Edited" by

Darick "DDS" Spears

The 21st Century Shakespears

ISBN 978-0692627297

**Printed in USA by DDS MediaWorks LLC./21st
Century Shakespears Publishing**

The Disclaimer

This book is a world full of poetry. Take a ride through

a deep train of thought. Darick will take each reader

on a very interesting journey through poetry. Please

enjoy.

More books available by Darick Spears on www.darickbooks.com

Dedication

This book is dedicated to all of those who appreciate life spoken through art and poetry.

We all have gifts, and letting God use you as a medium to get a message to people, is the a great feeling.

If you have further questions, contact DDS MediaWorks/21st Century Shakespears Publishing. Our regular business hours are Mon-Thurs. 8:30 am – 8 pm EST, and Friday 8:30 am – 5 pm. During these hours, you can reach us by phone, email or on-line chat. Outside of these hours, either call and leave a message or email us.

Phone: 414-628-0798

Email: darick@ddsmediaworks.com

Website: www.darickbooks.com

Author Biography

Darick "DDS" Spears, is an artist, producer, business owner, certified audio engineer with experience in video/film production, and an author. He graduated from Marquette University Milwaukee, WI with a Bachelors in Communications and Minor in Intermediary Business 2000-2005. He got his Masters Degree in Music Business at Columbia College Chicago, IL 2006-2008.

He also received his Associate Degree in Recording & Video Technology from Madison Media Institute 2010-2012.

Darick is a Business owner. DDS MediaWorks LLC, Milwaukee, WI: is a tri-media company that deals with music production, video production, and book writing/publishing.

Under the DDS Mediaworks umbrella, is a music label called Elevator Muzik Group. This music label was founded and is ran by Darick Spears. Log on to www.darickspears.com to check out new music.

*Finally, he has began a new book department called the 21ˢᵗ Century Shakespears Publishing Company. Known for the #1 Besteller book entitled :***The Diary of a stay-at-home Dad: My Journal Behind Bars***, & "**Sex Tell.**" This is the new installment called Poetic Confinement. A book full of poetry, written by Darick DDS Spears.*

Poetic Confinement

Poetic Confinement

Underneath the firmament it's all vanity,

In solitude I sit simply glancing meek!

Today I feel desolate because the walls don't say a

word.

I hum these tunes and sing these melodies,

They remain silent and I remain unheard.

Outside I wish to venture into the hills and in these

streets,

But mentally I'm a captive to words, exaggerations,

and beats.

I call this poetic confinement,

This prison has me trapped.

Religiously I pray to Christ to put me in that place

where dead Catholics nap.

Society becomes a foreign picture that Picasso

couldn't make clear,

To me, I don't exist because in my world there are no

mirrors.

Step By Step

Step by Step

Each step is an elevating reach.

An elevator speech.

The more I speak,

The more you learn about me.

Lord bring my feet to the ground of new faith.

Lead my feet to the ocean front,

The sound of new waves.

Take my steps to higher heights,

Where the eagles dwell,

Where there's a precious sound of silent nights.

The pain I've suffered is nothing compared to yours,

Yet I'm an heir of yours,

Walking up life's stairs where I declare it's more.

Let me reach new heights I've never seen,

Lord you are my everything!

Your perfection is a reflection no mirror has ever seen.

Forgive me if I have ever let fear shake my faith,

Lead my feet to sanctification and pure dedication.

Give me the Holy Ghost this very new day.

Now your spirit dwells in this broken vessel,

Risen to a holy level.

Now I am whole,

Now I am your soul,

Now my steps are only in your control.

Step by Step

Rose "99"

Rose "99"

A beautiful rose in a field of flowers surrounded by

shades of blue,

A soothing breeze and sprinkles of rain,

That nourish and bring forth a dew.

A glare of light from the toasted sun with just a tad

bit of shade,

Enough pedals to build a nest of security,

To keep the flowers from a world of hate.

Scenery in which you would die to see,

Hosted by a rose that's cute.

I am describing an important rose in my life,

And that rose I am describing is you!

Rose

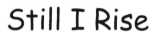

Still I Rise

Still I Rise

Shattered hearts and eyes filled with tears of hurt,

Have I failed to make you happy?

Or am I to you just a curse?

Ghettos and abandoned buildings filled with bodies

torn a part,

I can visualize mother in the room crying because the

death of her son has torn her heart.

My head drops in shame as I tell myself that my

mission is not complete,

I will face this adversity and I will never accept

defeat.

I've seen it all,

Bloodshed,

People's successes,

And tears of sorrow in people's eyes.

But I keep my focus and that's why I wrote this,

To remember that still I rise.

Still I rise.

The Product of Love

The Product of Love

Love devours all things,

Whether the sky is blue or not.

I can paint several pictures in life,

But love is where it stops.

It was brought to my attention inside another

dimension,

That I could change the world with love.

Create a life within a life,

That could demolish the hatred inside the wildest

thug.

I will breathe new air that could cleanse the soul, the

wild, the young, and the old.

I see visions of myself doing these things,

As if I were destined to be worth gold.

So, I multiply life times life,

And I came up with a bond full of brotherly love.

This is my image and there is no limit,

To the power to find the product of love.

The Product of Love.

I Ain't Trippin

Personally, life gets worser to me.

All the criticism I hear,

But ain't nobody perfect to me.

Thoughts race through my mind,

Is it a cure for this certain disease?

I don't understand so I get down on my knees.

Lord can you hear the cries of the youth?

Growing up with no parents,

Not having a clue in this world so they get involved

in crews.

Gangbangers and drug dealers,

Selling rocks on their blocks trying to be thug niggaz.

Searching for love inside a world full of cold-blooded

killers.

So we learn how to cope with with this certain

disease,

My brothaz make a come up by selling weed on these

streets.

Hopefully one day, some day, some way,

A cure will be put on the streets,

But until then I ain't trippin,

I just think it's a mental disease!

I Ain't Trippin

One Love

One Love

We all say goodbyes throughout our daily lives,

We make promises that that turn into hopeless lies,

And we all face demise.

Sacrifices we make just to stay ahead of the game,

Transactions we take to adjust to a life of not being

insane.

But in all that we do what's the future for you?

It ain't for me to tell ya,

I don't live the life you do.

We all make mistakes,

Nobody's perfect in this life.

I can't always be the serious person,

Nor can I always be polite.

But one thing we can learn before this crooked world

turns,

Is that we all live for a purpose,

So don't make this life worthless.

Watch for the snakes in the grass that slither and bite

at your feet.

Keep your head up high until you touch the sky,

And any goal you can reach.

One Love.

Shine

Shine

Face the dark times with a heart divine,

Constellations fell upon a galaxy,

Now freedom and wisdom are after me.

The aftermath furthered the prophecy,

Recommending that success be the stampede,

Shining divinely well-above and underneath.

Using the wrong ball for the right sport,

Feeling insecure because your dreams have come up short.

Speaking meekly to elders and priest,

In devotion to the heavenly father you seek.

Rewind the time as you sit and reminsce,

You've been through the worst pain but you have to learn how to survive the game.

With one direction you seek perfection with just one thing in mind,

That is to stand tall in all you do,

Shine.

Humble Be 4 a Nation

Humble Be 4 a Nation

Low-key,

Keep a deep profile.

No smiles because no growth has been in our town,

We've faced fortitude and we've been locked in

chains.

Before the slums can rise they must repent for the

violence and medicine in their veins.

When they hit us in our faces,

We must turn the other cheek.

Sounds twisted but we serve a God that's meek.

Low-key,

Keep a deep profile,

Humble before a nation,

With humility we bow!

Preschool Teens

Preschool Teens

A beautiful description of a girl that's afflicted,

Twisted in a world of ghetto boys and girls.

Priceless she moves her body and oddly it seems

righteous,

As the dice flips it splits creating a creature that's

lifeless.

Out in the late night she sees the rage and fights,

Searching for gold within a hood-driven soul.

Bold as she dreams of visions she's may not bestow.

As she stares in the air,

The scent of that weed kills her dreams and she feels

currency she needs.

Surrounded by sluts degrading themselves for more

means of wealth,

At the final hour she feels demise.

Because now she sees with her pussy and thighs.

She's stuck in a position where all she can do is

dream,

A beautiful description of a girl that's afflicted,

Preschool Teens!

Pussy is Power

Pussy is Power

You fail to believe that there is power in your jeans.

Two lips.

Don't trip, slip, and end up on top of a dick.

Covering it up with a thong and you got a nation

sprung,

But when it's wet you place your record on a whole

new song.

You got him buying you cars and all for what?

He would kill another brotha to protect your

scandulous butt.

Pussy is Power.

Keep it In The Family

Keep it in The Family

Lord you're probably wondering how my questions

come about?

But I don't understand why my voice of

misunderstanding can't shout.

I feel ashamed of the wicked's way of playing the

game.

Stuck in the mimic of a voice and a heart that's timid,

Just please tell me why my relationship with life is

ending?

From the intro to the exit it was nothing but hurt,

Daily seeking direction,

But I never found a natural drink to quench this

thirst.

Problems constantly mixed with unsolved mysteries,

Who could I ask?

You're the alpha and the omega,

You know what was the cause of this aftermath.

I feel so much hate in my heart and I am in a shady

position,

I want to just let it go,

But my conscience is drained from this sickness.

Lord you are my father and brother,

I don't want advice from another.

Please help me get through this insanity,

Sincerely Yours,

Darick DDS Spears.

Keep it in the Family!

A Christian Division: A World Renewed

A Christian Division: A World Renewed

Be ye strong my brethren,

Do not partake in the bows of the wicked.

Homies on the block stay strapped and bust back,

Before they do you like my cousin Willie.

Plant your seeds in the ground of righteousness and

they shall sprout up royal,

The cemetery is full of doped-up G's who to the game

stayed loyal.

For 40 days and 40 nights, Jesus was tempted of the

devil and he overcame,

In the ghetto it's "survival of the niggaz,"

They will slay you for your chains.

You ask me why I put these contrasting statements

together in sentences?

Because the world and the church are now in one

room, and they need a division.

Girls and Guys: A Stressing Eye

Girls and Guys: A Stressing Eye

Sleeping alone at night,

What a world!

Never heard of sharing and rarely felt like caring.

A man considered was considered a stranger,

Children weren't immune to your baring.

Never was it fair,

Not in your sight.

Girls and Guys: A stressing Eye

A man alone can't be very strong,

His meadows are vessels filled with few songs.

Women to him are foreign,

He wouldn't even know how to speak to Lauren.

His inner storage is packed with tears and helpless

fears,

Still stuck in position and can't change gears.

Still stuck on hopeless lies,

Girls and Guys: A stressing Eye

Sucka 4 Luv II

Sucka 4 Luv II

Gone like the wind,

A heart devastated.

Divided like a thin line between love and hatred.

Flawless!

A petite uniform accompanied by two superb pieces.

Lips, hips, and lovely tits,

Check out my organized thesis.

Well-prepared for this deposition,

The maids intuition wasn't misunderstanding this

master's position.

Viscious in this relationship,

No patience so quick to collide with external

fragrances.

Affairs and future repairs were the price of a few

minutes of ruin,

For this couple was not prudent in their wrong

doings.

One day their fate was brought in with the sunlight,

Both eyes were opened and they knew something

wasn't right.

Gone like the wind,

Their love began to transcend.

Oddly,

They were again reunited under a love spell hot like

fire.

Sucka 4 Luv II

My Lady's Sidekick

Frigidly I dealt with the situation,

It had me anticipating nothing but pure devastation.

Once upon a time I had a good relationship,

But today I was stuck in yesterday's separation.

Snakes in the grass working their way to the dirt on

the pavement.

Still stuck on page two trying to get to three,

But my lady's sidekick just got a hold of me,

Wearing the finest longerie had my faithfulness bent

to a degree.

At night time while my lady would be at work from

six to twelve,

I was so caught up in the moment you could say I

was in the depths of hell.

From the bottom step to the top step,

Nothing but sweat and sex.

Guilt trips filled our bellies until one day I broke the

yoke,

When I told my lady's sidekick to hit the door.

Too Personal For Thee

Too Personal For Thee

That's my pet peeve,

Comparing me to another person.

Nothing could possibly get worst.

Talking behind my back and smiling in my face.

Looking at my lady's body and ridiculing my race.

Telling me that I won't ever be nothing.

Talking about you're from the hood when you ain't

never heard a gun busting.

Representing a false nation and showing fake love.

Always quick to talk about somebody and no one

made you the judge!

Too personal for me,

To be continued,

That's my pet peeve.

Dear Sport

Dear Sport

10 seconds left,

They pass me the ball and the crowd gets hype.

I take it up the court and cross over from left to right,

Take a second to breathe,

It's only eight seconds left.

Time is going by so fast and I gotta make a decision,

But first I have to catch my breath.

I see the center but he's covered,

The shooting guard's blocked and so are the others.

I got 5 seconds left and there's only one thing I can do,

Though I do it best, being DDS,

I had to shoot.

The clock was at two seconds and I then took a deep

breath,

Once I took the shot with one second left on the clock.

All I could remember was hearing the crowd shout,

While the commentator yelled "He's hot."

Dear Sport.

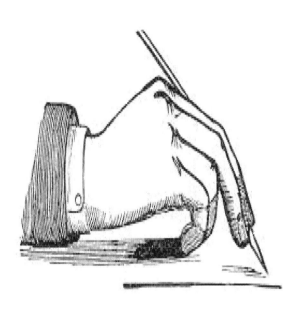

It Sounds like A Good Start

It Sounds like a Good Start (Explicit Poetry)

It was a perfect breeze and it was dark in the east,
The clouds were deceased and there were no cops on
the streets.
The gangbangers were all at this party on the west,
That just left you babydoll, with this nigga DDS.
I'm at the sex store buying up some products for this
trip,
Jumped back in my benz with ends,
Now it's time to satisfy my dick.
Picture this!
I can visualize your sexy lips, breast, and thick hips,
Got my hormones bumping louder than the bass in
my whip.
I pull up in your drive way and right away I can see
you at the door,
Titties out, and I can hear your pussy shout,
Because your panties are on the floor.
Big daddy is home,

You're singing that song,

I feel like it's time to start class.

I walked through the path,

Thrashing and dashing,

Cuz I'm gonna wax that ass.

I open the door and throw my clothes on the floor,

Don't give a damn about the lights,

Tonight I'm the slut and you're the whore.

Sounds like a Good Start.

A Weary Picture: But Still There's Hope

A Weary Picture: But Still There's Hope!

Though the caskets be filled deep,

Times the moments wouldn't sleep.

I can still visualize a moment in time where all

brothers and sisters can see the light.

Though my enemies might not forsee delight,

Disaster isn't quite the sight.

Picture heaven on earth,

Seven before six.

A day when you can humble yourself and wipe the

dirt off your neighbor's kicks.

A day when there are empty penitenuaries.

Picture success and a sense of hope in the words that

I've wrote.

It's a weary portrait but still there's always hope.

Integrity

Integrity

I was once told,

Stand bold.

Toe even with each toe.

Let no scandal mold a story that you have told.

Be direct,

Let truth be a reflection of your soul,

Smile with your chest out and set yourself a goal.

When adversity ascends,

You defend your territory.

Listen to the words coming from the son of Dennis

and Lori.

This is a saint tale,

Not another Westside story.

Trust me when I say that no man becomes a threat

until he is important.

Because with low self-esteem there is no progression

it seems,

Speak with a tongue of honesty,

Sometimes it is healthy to close your eyes and dream.

But when you wake up and remember that reality is a

real thing,

Hate none but love all,

Even the one's you would consider a friend but they

pray for your downfall.

Keep Jesus first that has been my thesis since birth,

Respect all creatures that walk the earth.

And never give up,

Keep your words with sincerity,

And most important,

Keep integrity.

Lady of the Eve

Lady of the Eve

One night of passion,

Pure satisfacrion,

All of this was in the midst of late night traffic.

Years prior, on her butt my eyes were fastened.

I never thought I would feel the back of her gluteus

maximus.

Her gentle massage would convey in my mind a

naked mirage,

As she stroked my pole my hormones were awaken

to live.

Did she know I had been waiting for this moment

since we first laid eyes on each other?

I can still hear her words,

"hit me from the back, but first put on a rubber."

My shock invaded my cock, and within minutes this

feeling would stop.

As I pushed my love inside,

Her butt was in the air and her head inside the

pillows eyes.

When we finished she departed with our secret,

And in the wilderness of her memory she will forever

keep it.

Our Covenant Pt. 1

Our Covenant Pt. 1

A bond between God and a nation,

Abraham,

An individual.

Which do you symbolize?

A body,

A mind,

Or an open heart?

Choose this day and play your part.

Our covenant.

We agree to seek one in the skies above,

The one located in the high rise of the firmament.

Whose grace is sufficient,

Who will keep us determined,

Our covenant.

A bond from rebirth til earthly death,

Until we are resurrected with a taste of glory's breath.

A journey I've found, and I've met,

Lord Jesus your covenant I accept.

Our Covenant.

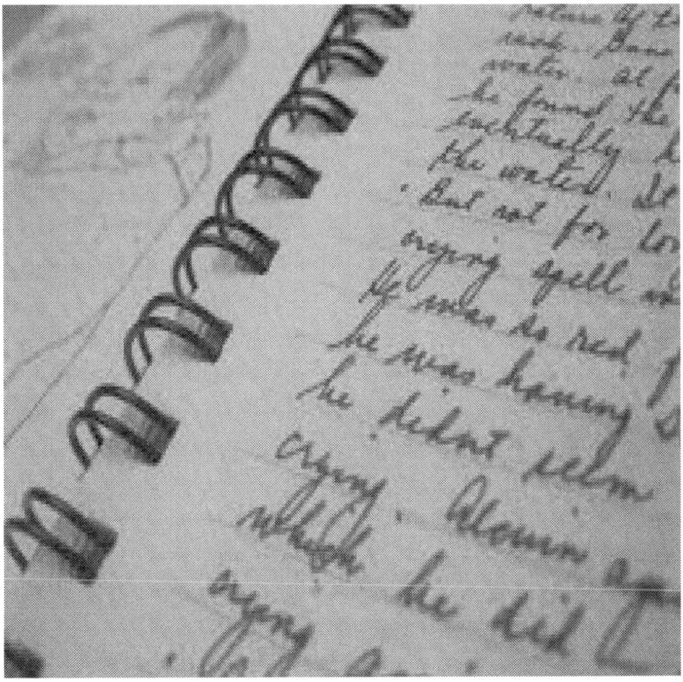

Poverty of The Mind

Poverty of the Mind

Some have poor choice in words,

Flaring emotions.

Provoking gestures,

Daring notions,

Others are blessed peaceful insight like the sight of

the calm ocean.

Hard to think about the captives of history, when you

are a victim yourself.

Viewing yourself as a miniscule element in the eyes of

individuals with wealth.

Society cultivates our minds with books written in

riddles,

You want to change the world but end up in the

middle.

To be ignorant is not to know.

To be stupid is to know and not make a move,

But some still find themselves dancing to life's

confusing groove.

Knowing too much can provoke fear to surface,

Spread the word and let it be heard by doing a

service.

Let not your heart be troubled and stay on your

grind,

Because without understanding we all develop

poverty of the mind.

Poverty of the Mind

Be Ye Strong

Be Ye Strong

A low point in your life,

A lost in your eyes but it is a gain in Christ's.

The essence of stress,

The unknown has chased your mind out of it's desk.

A student of truth,

Abused in my youth.

Mentally,

But I guess it was meant to be.

I heard your daughter has found peace,

While we dwell on the Earth fighting the beast.

I'm proud of you so stay strong,

Remain on the track that Jesus has placed you on.

And remember,

You are never alone.

I'm here.

"This poem is dedicated to anyone who has lost a

love one. Stay strong and keep your faith in

Jesus."_DDS

Watch Me

Watch Me

My life pro-rated,

Taken down a notch.

The plots of my civilization,

The economy's way of infuriating an individual.

But I tell you that it is my smile that's worth more

than the riches of the world,

It is my pride.

My smile is my natural resource,

It is my gift from Jesus.

When I speak of pride it is not of conceit,

It is the confidence that lies inside of me.

My life's value is now upgraded,

Taken up a notch.

The plots of the heavens,

To uplift every soul until we reach the potential in

which we are destined.

I am the evidence.

Now watch me.

The Perils of the Earth

The Perils of the Earth (Wilderness)

Things written in books,

Scrolls overlooked.

Man-made theories spoken while people follow the

words of a crook,

The Apocalyse.

The unveiling,

Tales being told in the land of the telling.

<u>The Perils of the Earth.</u>

In this dark wilderness I've held discussions with

elders,

Not swayed by gnostic theories,

Only with wisdom and understanding do we use the

B.I.B.L.E. As our roadmap to get into heaven.

Clearly,

Every day is a personal and spiritual journey,

Seeking Christ for answers to questions that fog up

our mirrors,

<u>The Perils of the Earth.</u>

The lies, the injustices, the hate,

The unknown, the separation between the real and

the fake.

Men's love for themselves,

5 Percent Nations,

Babylon's evilness,

Israel's fate.

Wars between religions,

The real versus the fake.

A search for the Anti-Christ,

But time is not on our side.

Take a walk with me through this wilderness,

The Apocalypse,

The unveiling,

Are you down for the ride?

<u>The Perils of the Earth.</u>

Try Loving

Try Loving

My nerves dissecting,

Fluctuating.

Earlier glad and now mad,

Two ordeals.

The feelings shared between two love birds,

War on a battlefield,

Candace.

My love name seems to mean light,

But sometimes when we part I feel dark,

Angry.

Strangely I still love you,

How can you put up with man that is troubled?

Stressed and even though I am blessed,

Some things in life are hard to digest.

The fake friends,

My pockets which are deprived of ends,

But you stuck with me, and therefore this argument is

over,

Let's make amends.

"Life is too short to hold grudges. Sometimes we

don't even know why we are fighting. Today try

forgiving and loving."_DDS

Candy Love

Candy Love

In my daydreams I may sing,

I may say things like,

"I got a guitar and I wanna play these strings."

Look at what this weight brings,

Thoughts racing like my heartbeat after a crazy

dream.

But my heart often beats to the rhythm of your hips,

And sweat builds up as I visualize you who is the

mother of my kids.

My little black sexy monster,

What God has put together let no man take asunder.

What is this, just another day?

Naw, it's just another way to say that you're all that,

An employer that I wouldn't hesitate to call back,

I need a job!

And I know I can mean more to you than a cash wad,

All these sexual thoughts I have to stop,

Or maybe not.

Because you're my wife.

I Speak with Passion

I Speak with Passion

A new environment,

Frozen gestures.

A culture shock scene,

Where forever seemed forever.

Isolated and driven forward like my mission so I go

hard.

I keep pushing myself to the limits just like the

Women's Suffrage,

I deserve rights too.

How would you feel if I told you that I didn't like

you?

Desperate I yearn to manifest my dreams into reality,

A place where men witness their fatality.

Their faith is lacking, but see,

I won't fail.

I got the Holy Ghost to attest to this.

A confession,

I will never lose because Jesus,

Through you I find my justice.

Beauty

Beauty

Beauty is her name,

O what a fame.

Her smile of sunshine cuts through the rain,

A dear friend?

Someone else's love?

Whatever the case is you were sent from above,

A compliment I give you.

Beauty is your dominant issue,

This is from the outside looking at the physical.

A pure heart?

Maybe insecurity?

Whatever the scenario in my eyes you are truly,

Beauty.

"Inspired by all the beautiful women in the world.

Stay beautiful, confident, and never settling for less."

_ DDS

I Have a Purpose: Without Measure

I Have a Purpose: Without Measure

Wealth have I none,

But I have a smile full of riches.

In this wilderness I roam,

Wondering what is my mission?

Nervous and confined to each step I take,

In the depths of solitude.

I become more introspective each day,

My temper,

My dreams of being an emperor,

Ruling a world that is non-existent,

Leaving the hot devil to freeze alone in the chilling

winter.

Time has become my enemy,

The truth of the matter is the night time offends me.

No sunshine,

Nothing but storage sounds and a stomach that is

empty

It's hard being a saint.

In a wilderness surrounded by foreign sounds,

Non-believers that doubt a faith that could move a

mountain off of the ground.

But I feel I have a purpose,

To one day be perfect,

Christ died in exchange for me to do a service.

A word of truth,

An intermediary for you.

A lost soul with a feeling of misunderstood,

Without a knowing of what to do,

My niggaz know that one thing is true,

To live for Christ is worth it.

Be a servant.

For we all have purpose.

Solitude II

Solitude II

Silence froze my skies,

A high rise of mental anguish.

My garden had no precipitation,

Therefore, its progress was stagnant.

Remnant hymns formulated tunes that crickets would

usually make.

Stress I must intake.

<u>Solitude.</u>

Feeling the sting of silence,

Could it be like the death of biblical Minister

Stephen?

Being stoned watching my own demise,

While staring at my Gods throne.

A world full of curiosity,

Wondering is there any one on the outside?

Standing in the heart of void,

<u>Solitude.</u>

Every man, woman, boy, girl must one day face

themselves,

All alone a victim of silence.

Dancing with visions that are inviting,

Lust, dreams, and nightmares,

Only to wake up and realize that it is right there.

<u>Solitude.</u>

-

Made in the USA
San Bernardino, CA
30 April 2016